My Little Golden Book About

Dolly Parton

By Deborah Hopkinson

Illustrated by Monique Dong

The editors would like to thank T. Duane Gordon,
editor and publisher of Dollymania.net, for his assistance
in the preparation of this book.

A GOLDEN BOOK • NEW YORK

Text copyright © 2021 by Deborah Hopkinson
Cover art and interior illustrations copyright © 2021 by Monique Dong
All rights reserved. Published in the United States by Golden Books, an imprint of Random
House Children's Books, a division of Penguin Random House LLC, 1745 Broadway, New
York, NY 10019. Golden Books, A Golden Book, A Little Golden Book, the G colophon, and the
distinctive gold spine are registered trademarks of Penguin Random House LLC.
rhcbooks.com
Educators and librarians, for a variety of teaching tools, visit us at RHTeachersLibrarians.com
Library of Congress Control Number: 2021930920
ISBN 978-0-593-30685-7 (trade) — ISBN 978-0-593-30686-4 (ebook)
Printed in the United States of America
20 19 18 17 16 15 14 13 12 11

Dolly Rebecca Parton was born on January 19, 1946, in a one-room cabin in the foothills of the Smoky Mountains in Tennessee. Dolly was the fourth of twelve children.

Each morning, her daddy went off to work carrying his lunch in a battered old dinner bucket. Her mama cooked and cleaned from sunup to dark, then mended clothes and stitched quilts by the light of a kerosene lamp. Her family might have been poor, but Dolly's life was rich with music and love.

Dolly and her sisters and brothers made
their own fun. From the time she was little,
Dolly pretended she was a star. She perched
on the woodpile or stood on the cabin porch
to perform for the chickens, the ducks, and her
little brothers and sisters. Sometimes, though,
her audience just crawled off or waddled away.

One chilly fall, Dolly's mama made her a special coat from colorful scraps of cloth. Kids at school called it a bunch of rags. Their teasing made Dolly sad, but she wouldn't take off her coat. She knew her mama had sewn each tiny stitch with love.

When she grew up, Dolly told this story in her famous song "Coat of Many Colors."

Dolly has always loved butterflies, flitting and flying so free. One day when she was a child, she followed a bright-orange monarch and got lost in the woods.

Suddenly, she heard a bell. It was the family cow, Bessie! Dolly ran over and grabbed the leather collar her daddy had made for the animal. Dolly hung on tight, stumbling through briars and bushes as Bessie led her all the way home.

Dolly is a bit like a beautiful butterfly herself—gentle and colorful. She lights up the stage in her fancy outfits. And she enjoys showing off her gorgeous, glamorous wigs.

Even though she's all grown up, Dolly still makes her own fun.

Dolly was only ten years old when she began appearing on local radio and television shows.

At first, she felt nervous. Then she took a big breath and sang from her heart, just like at home on the woodpile. Her dazzling smile and clear, high voice charmed everyone.

Dolly was on TV before her family even owned one!

As a girl, Dolly set her sights high. She dreamed of singing onstage at the famous Grand Ole Opry in Nashville. From there, people all over America would hear her on their radios.

"I want to be on the Opry!"

Dolly was only thirteen when country music legend Johnny Cash introduced her at the Grand Ole Opry. This was the big time!

Dolly stepped up to the microphone. She sang for God and for her mama and daddy—and for all the people who believed in her.

Everyone loved Dolly!

At her high school graduation, Dolly declared that she was going to Nashville to become a star. People laughed. But that only made her more determined to succeed.

The very next day, she hopped on a bus to
Nashville with just her guitar, her songs, and a
few belongings packed into three paper bags.

On her first day in town, outside the Wishy Washy Laundromat, Dolly met a handsome young man named Carl Dean. It was love at first sight.

Two years later, Dolly and Carl decided to marry. They had a small, simple wedding and have been together ever since.

Although they never had children of their own, Dolly and Carl opened their hearts and home to help raise some of Dolly's younger brothers and sisters.

Years later, for their fiftieth wedding anniversary, Dolly and Carl decided to make up for their simple wedding. They married again, and this time, Dolly wore a shimmering gown. Then they got into their RV and went on a camping trip.

After Dolly and Carl first got married, Dolly kept working hard. Before long, some of her songs became number-one hits. She started to win big awards, including top female country singer of the year! But Dolly didn't limit herself to one kind of music. She made a big splash in pop music, too.

Since Dolly loved performing, one day she decided to try acting. Her first film, called *9 to 5,* is about women like her, who work hard for success. Dolly wrote the movie's title song, which became a huge hit.

Dolly never seems to run out of ideas—she has written more than five thousand songs!

It's no wonder Dolly's list of awards for songwriting, music, and acting fills many pages. She has changed country music. She has made television shows and written books, too. Dolly is one of the most honored American performers of all time.

Along with being a creative person, Dolly is a successful businesswoman. Each year, people flock to Dollywood, her theme park in the Smoky Mountains. Dollywood has brought jobs to the area, and it honors the music and traditions of the people who live there.

Dolly also helps in other ways. Out of love for her father, who never got the chance to learn to read, she began Dolly Parton's Imagination Library. Each month, Imagination Library sends free books to more than a million preschool children in America and in other countries around the world.

"Faith, hope, and love are the three most important words in my life!"

Like the butterfly she once followed as a child, Dolly has traveled far in her life. She began by singing on a woodpile. Now the whole world is her stage. She has never been afraid to be herself, or to raise her voice to help others.

Dolly Parton is like no one else. And one thing is certain:

Everyone loves Dolly!